HIGH-TECH MILITARY WEAPONS

JET FIGHTER: THE HARRIER AV-8B

Julie Beyer

Children's Press
High Interest Books
A Division of Grolier Publishing
New York / London / Hong Kong / Sydney
Danbury, Connecticut

To my husband

Contributing Editors: Mark Beyer and Rob Kirkpatrick
Book Design: Michael DeLisio

Photo Credits: Cover © Robin Ashead; The Military Picture Library/Corbis; p. 5, 26 © Peter Russell; The Military Picture Library/Corbis; p. 6, 9, 17, 36 © George Hall/Corbis; p. 10 © John H. Clark/Corbis; p. 13 © DefenseLink; p. 14 © Paul Almasy/Corbis; p. 20 © Clive Newton; The Military Picture Library/ Corbis; p. 23 © Leif Skoogfors/Corbis; p. 24, 30, 33, 39 © Corbis; p. 28 © Martin McKenzie; The Military Picture Library/Corbis; p. 34, 18 © Aero Graphics, Inc./Corbis; p. 42, 43 Harrier Illustrations by Michael DeLisio

Visit Children's Press on the Internet at:
http://publishing.grolier.com

Library of Congress Cataloging-in-Publication Data

Beyer, Julie.
Jet fighter: the Harrier AV-8B / by Julie Beyer
p. cm. – (High-tech military weapons)
Includes bibliographical references and index.
ISBN 0-516-23340-8 (lib. bdg.) – ISBN 0-516-23540-0 (pbk.)
1. Harrier (Jet fighter plane)—Juvenile literature. [1. Harrier (Jet fighter plane)] I. Title. II. Series.

UG1242.F5B474 2000
623.7'464—dc21

00-022695

Printed in the United States of America.
1 2 3 4 5 6 7 8 9 10 R 05 04 03 02 01 00

CONTENTS

INTRODUCTION

Have you ever wondered what you would get if you crossed a jet airplane with a helicopter? British airplane engineers wondered, and they built the Harrier! The Harrier can fly as fast as a jet airplane. It also can take off and land the way a helicopter can. Both of these things have made it an important aircraft to Great Britain, the United States, and many other countries.

Britain's Royal Air Force first used the Harrier in 1969. The U.S. Marine Corps began to use the Harrier AV-8A in 1976. In 1979, Britain's Royal Navy first used the Sea Harrier aboard their aircraft carriers. By 1984, the U.S. Marine Corps was using still another version of the Harrier, the AV-8B. No matter which model we talk about or what country is using it, the Harrier is a really special aircraft. No other airplane can do the things a Harrier can do.

The Harrier is part jet, part helicopter.

CHAPTER 1

A UNIQUE AIRPLANE

ACTS LIKE A HELICOPTER, LOOKS LIKE A JET

Have you ever seen a helicopter take off? It goes straight up, or vertical, before it goes forward. Helicopters have huge blades, called rotors, on top of them. Motors make the rotors spin faster and faster. As the rotors spin, air is pushed down. Then the air bounces back and pushes up the helicopter. The Harrier can do this too, but it does not have rotors on top of it the way a helicopter does. It has wings that are fixed in place. The Harrier also has four nozzles on it.

The Harrier can go straight upward when it takes off, just as a helicopter can.

The Harrier is what is called a V/STOL (Vertical/Short Take-Off and Landing) aircraft. V/STOL makes the Harrier very useful. Unlike other jet fighters, the Harrier does not need a runway to take off. Even if the pilot is in the middle of a jungle, the Harrier can take off almost vertically. However, if the plane is on an aircraft carrier in the middle of the Atlantic Ocean, it can use a short runway for takeoff. The Harrier also can take off using a regular runway, just as other jets can.

TAKING OFF

The pilot sits in the main part of a jet fighter's body. This also is where the engine is located. A jet fighter's body is called the fuselage. The wings and tail are attached to the fuselage. On the Harrier jet fighter, there are four jet nozzles on the fuselage. These nozzles direct the engine's jet power.

Fast-spinning fans that push air out of

The Harrier's engines are attached to its body, or fuselage.

them create jet power. Jet power is directed behind regular jets. This power pushes the jet forward down the runway. When the jet reaches a certain speed (more than 150 miles per hour), it can take off and fly.

The Harrier is able to use jet power differently. The nozzles on the Harrier can be turned. They can point backward or straight down. The nozzles are moved in certain directions depending on what the pilot wants the aircraft to do.

Vertical takeoff pushes the plane straight up.

If the pilot wants to take off vertically, he or she moves a lever so that the nozzles point down. With the nozzles pointed at the ground, the power from the engines lifts the airplane straight up. When the Harrier is in the air, the pilot begins to turn the rear nozzles to point backward. This makes the plane move forward. The nozzles turn slowly so that the plane is steady in the air. The two rear nozzles turn backward. This moves the plane forward. The front nozzles continue to point downward to maintain lift. The plane gains speed as the rear nozzles are turned all the way backward. Now the plane is really moving fast. It is almost flying forward under its own jet power. Then the front nozzles are turned to point backward. When they are pointed backward, the Harrier can fly straight. The plane is then moving fast enough to stay in the air using its wings. The wings keep a plane in the air by lifting it as it moves forward.

If you have ever seen a Harrier take off, it is almost like watching a flying saucer in an old UFO movie. The plane's engine starts up and the plane lifts straight up before it goes forward. This amazing ability is what makes the Harrier a big hit at many air shows. The U.S. Marine Corps loves to show off this spectacular machine.

HOVERING

The Harrier is unique in its ability to hover. Hovering means the plane can fly in place. By hovering, a plane can come almost to a complete stop before it lands. This is a much safer way to land than the way other airplanes land. Other planes fly to the ground and land while moving at almost 200 miles per hour before they eventually come to a stop.

Hovering lets the Harrier pilot be in more control of the airplane during the landing. The pilot is able to see the ground more clearly. He or she can react to danger on the ground more quickly. That means the Harrier can fire its guns at the enemy while landing. Other fighter jets are moving too fast to fire while they land.

SIDEBAR

The Harrier is the world's first jet fighter used in battle that can take off and land vertically! The first hovering flight by a Hawker-Siddeley Harrier was made in England on August 31, 1966.

The Harrier works well on an aircraft carrier because it doesn't need a runway to take off or land.

52
26
VI
DIV
LHA3

CHAPTER 2

BUILDING THE HARRIER JET FIGHTER

A company called Hawker-Siddeley Aviation designed the first Harrier. Hawker-Siddeley is now a part of British Aerospace in England. Britain began testing this type of aircraft around 1960. By 1969, the modern-day Harrier jet fighter was flying. The British Royal Air Force began to use the Harrier.

An American company soon became interested in the Harrier. McDonnell Douglas began working with British Aerospace around 1975. The two companies helped each other to develop the Harrier now known as the AV-8B Harrier II.

The Rolls-Royce company built engines such as this one for the Harrier jet fighter.

The Harrier weighs about 13,000 pounds when it is empty. It can weigh more than 29,000 pounds when it is fully loaded with fuel, weapons, and crew. However, the Harrier cannot take off vertically when it weighs 29,000 pounds. The Harrier can't weigh more than 19,185 pounds for vertical takeoff. A vertical takeoff uses more fuel. More fuel adds weight to the aircraft. The more fuel that is needed to fly the plane, the less weight can be used for weapons. Pilots think about aircraft weight before they fly any mission. They make sure they will not run out of weapons or fuel while in enemy territory.

The Harrier is more than 46 feet long. Its wingspan (length from the end of one wing to the end of the other wing) is 30 feet. The plane is 11 feet high. The Harrier usually flies at a speed of 690 miles per hour. It can zoom to faster than 1,000 miles per hour.

The Harrier's powerful jet nozzles give it the thrust it needs to take off.

The Harrier jet fighter uses a Rolls-Royce Pegasus engine. This engine divides its power between the four jet nozzles connected to the plane's fuselage. A lot of thrust (jet power) is needed to lift a plane straight up off the ground. The Pegasus must be a big, powerful engine to lift this jet fighter.

The Harrier uses only one-third the amount of fuel that other jets use during takeoff. When a jet fighter is sent on a mission, it must fly to the battle and then back. The amount of fuel it uses determines how

The Harrier's fuel supply allows it to reach battles up to 600 miles away.

far it can fly. When on a mission, fighter jets fly quickly to the battle. After they attack an enemy, they fly quickly back to base. The flying distance to a battle and back to base is called a plane's strike distance. A Harrier's strike distance is 600 miles. That means it can fly 600 miles to a battle, and then back to base. When a Harrier is not in battle, it can fly more than 2,000 miles on a full tank.

CHAPTER 3

THE HARRIER IN COMBAT

BRITAIN

The first military group to use the Harrier was Britain's Royal Air Force. They were the first to fly a Harrier across the Atlantic Ocean. The flight was in 1969, from Northolt in England to Floyd Bennett Field, New York.

Sea Harrier

In 1978, Britain's Royal Air Force first used the Sea Harrier. This type of Harrier jet fighter was made for use on aircraft carriers. When Sea Harriers take off from an aircraft carrier, they

The Harrier often uses a ramp when taking off from an aircraft carrier.

usually use a ramp. The plane races along the short runway and launches itself off the ramp. This takes less time to get the plane into the air. It doesn't need to use so much engine power. Then the plane can gain power and fly more easily. The engine power takes over to give the plane enough speed to fly.

The ramp allows the plane to use less fuel than would be used in a vertical takeoff. If the plane carries less fuel, then it is able to carry more weapons. By 1979, the British Royal Navy used Sea Harriers on its aircraft carriers.

The first time Sea Harriers were used in combat was April 1982. Argentina, a South American country, had invaded Britain's Falkland Islands. Argentina claimed the islands. Britain and Argentina went to war. In that war, twenty-eight Sea Harriers flew combat missions. A total of thirty-eight Harriers were sent to the South Atlantic to retake the Falkland Islands from the Argentineans.

Because of bad weather, most fighter jets could not fly from British aircraft carriers. The seas were too rough for planes to take off and land normally. However, Harriers are not normal jet fighters. The Harriers were able to use their V/STOL abilities to get in the air and fight.

Some of the planes that the British Harriers were fighting against were French-built Mirages. Mirages are very fast airplanes.

However, British Harrier pilots shot down thirty-one Argentine jets. Not a single Harrier was lost during the war.

UNITED STATES

The U.S. Army, Navy, Air Force, and Marines use Harrier jet fighters. The Marine Corps uses the most Harriers. The Marine Corps is often on missions that are perfect for the Harrier. That's because the Marines often start missions from aircraft carriers. They also fight many battles in jungles and cities. Each of these places is ideal for using Harrier jet fighters. Harriers can launch from carriers in almost any weather. A runway can't be easily built in a jungle. And cities are very crowded. But being close to the action is no problem for a Harrier. It can lift vertically and get to a danger spot quickly. Then it can return and not need a runway to land. A pilot couldn't ask for more!

Because it can hover, the Harrier can take off in thick jungle areas.

In January 1971, the Marine Corps got its first Harriers. The U.S. Marine Corps first used Harriers in combat during the 1991 Gulf War. Harrier pilots carried out night strikes in the desert. They also helped ground troops to fight. They went into an area first and fired on enemy targets. Afterward, the ground troops marched in and finished the attack.

9133

CHAPTER 4

WEAPONS, DEFENSE, AND TACTICS

The Harrier uses many different weapons. A Harrier can carry up to 5 tons of weapons. The Harrier carries its weapons under its wings. These weapons include different kinds of missiles and bombs. When fully loaded, the Harrier can carry up to eight different kinds of missiles. It also can carry up to 4,000 pounds of bombs. The pilot fires the weapons from the cockpit.

THE COCKPIT

The cockpit of the Harrier is very high-tech. It is where the pilot flies the plane and where he

The Harrier can carry up to two tons of bombs.

aims and fires its weapons. Most Harriers have just one seat in the cockpit. But some do have seats for a pilot and a copilot. All Harrier cockpits have ejection seats so that the pilot can eject from the plane if needed.

The pilot gets information about both his own aircraft and enemy vehicles from what is called the head up display (HUD). The HUD is an electronic device that works like a movie projector. It projects information onto the inside of the windshield. The HUD allows the pilot to see information while flying the plane. This helps him concentrate on flying rather than looking down at dials and instruments.

Radar (Radio Detecting And Ranging) is what gives information to a digital weapon aiming computer (WAC) and the HUD. Radar sends electronic signals into the air. These signals bounce off things that are in the air or on the ground. The signals return to the radar instrument and show up on the HUD.

The cockpit has a special radar system that helps the pilot in battle.

The Harrier carries air-to-air and air-to-ground missiles.

The HUD can be used to track the enemy. It even can help the pilot to aim weapons and lock onto enemy targets.

MISSILES

Missiles are weapons that are shot at targets. Missiles are guided either by radar or by video guidance systems. Either way, missiles are fired from the plane from distances of up to 15 miles from their targets.

AIM-9L Sidewinder

The AIM-9L Sidewinder missile is an air-to-air missile. It is used against enemy fighter planes. The Sidewinder is aimed using radar guidance and targeting. When the pilot locates an enemy plane on his radar, he locks onto it. He does this by hitting a button. This identifies the target and holds its radar connection. When the plane gets close enough, the pilot fires the missile. The missile follows the plane and explodes when it hits the plane.

AGM-65 Maverick

The Maverick is an air-to-ground missile. It can be used to destroy buildings, railroads, ships, and enemy radar stations. The Maverick

is guided by a video guidance system. Before the missile is fired, the pilot can view the target on a video screen. When the Maverick is fired, it flies toward the target. The pilot can see the target getting closer as the Maverick flies toward it. The pilot can even steer the missile from the cockpit. The ability to steer this missile in midair makes the Maverick a deadly weapon.

BOMBS

Unlike missiles, bombs are dropped from planes as they fly over their targets. However, bombs do have guidance systems that help to aim them at their targets.

Snake-Eye

The U.S. Marine Corps' Harriers use a 1,000-pound Snake-Eye bomb. The Snake-Eye has a laser-guided computer in its nose. A laser (intense light) beam is fixed on the target by

The Harrier can cause some major damage with its weapons!

a soldier on the ground, by the Harrier pilot, or by another airplane. As the bomb falls to the ground, the laser reflects off the target. This reflection aims the bomb at the target. Snake-Eye bombs are very effective because they carry 1,000 pounds of explosives. Their accuracy makes them deadly.

EARLY WARNING SYSTEM

If a Harrier has a problem during flight, the centralized warning system (CWS) activates. Using an electronic voice, the CWS warns the pilot of problems with the engine, altitude, or weapons. During battle, if a pilot is dangerously close to the ground, the CWS will call out the signals "Altitude" or "Pull Up!" The CWS has saved many pilots' lives with such warnings. Pilots have a chance to correct the problem or fly the plane away from danger before disaster strikes.

Military techs prepare the bombs before placing them in the Harrier.

FIGHTING TACTICS

The Harrier is ideal for the U.S. Marines because it can take off easily from both land and ships. Britain and the United States have worked together to improve the Harrier by making it lighter, more fuel efficient, and able to carry more weapons. Today's Harrier is a much better plane than the first Harrier model.

The Harrier can fly from almost any level patch of ground. It also can take off from a concealed location. It can operate from remote areas on almost any terrain (ground). Its advantages are mobility, flexibility, and surprise.

Viffing

The Harrier can get away from the enemy because of a maneuver called viffing. (Vectoring In Forward Flight). This means the pilot can move the nozzles and quickly slow down the plane.

The Harrier is a special fighter plane.

Picture this dogfight in your mind: An enemy that is flying about 700 miles per hour is coming up behind a Harrier. The Harrier pilot uses his viffing ability and slows down really fast. Viffing is like slamming on the brakes of a car while it is moving along a highway. The enemy plane, which cannot viff, flies right past the Harrier. Then the Harrier pilot quickly speeds up and goes on the attack.

Viffing has other advantages, too. Viffing lets the pilot make tight turns. Thanks to viffing, Harriers also can pull out of dives (flying straight down) very quickly. This move confuses the enemy about where the Harrier is going. You can see how viffing makes the Harrier a very flexible, tricky fighter.

In flight trials, the Harrier was tested against supersonic fighters like the F-4 Phantom, F-14 Tomcat, and F-15 Eagle. Viffing helped the Harrier to beat these other

The Harrier can make sudden turns at high speeds.

planes. About 95 percent of the test-flights resulted in "kills" for the Harrier.

Hovering

The Harrier's ability to hover makes this jet fighter a deadly weapon. Hovering can help a Harrier to destroy an enemy during a mission. Regular fighter planes must always fly forward. Their speed can take them out of a battle with an enemy on the ground. For example, if a pilot detects an enemy within a jungle, he must fly past the enemy and come back to fight. The Harrier can stop itself quickly and hover. While hovering, the Harrier can turn from side to side or around in a circle. It can fire its weapons at targets that might otherwise have escaped.

THE HARRIER IN BATTLE

The Harrier is not meant to be a war-winner. As used by the United States and Britain, the

This enemy vehicle was unlucky to meet the Harrier in battle.

Harrier supports small missions. It is a perfect jet fighter to use for gaining control of a small area. Such areas are important places in a larger battle.

There are many advantages that a Harrier has over other fighter jets. A Harrier does not need a large airfield to take off or land. Harriers can hide in camouflage (disguise) tents close to the fighting. They are ready to leap into action at a moment's notice.

The flexibility of the Harrier proves its value. The future of the Harrier is secure. In the years to come, the Harrier jet fighters will improve their ability to fight against warring nations.

The Harrier can take off
for battle at a moment's notice.

The Harrier AV-8B

Side view

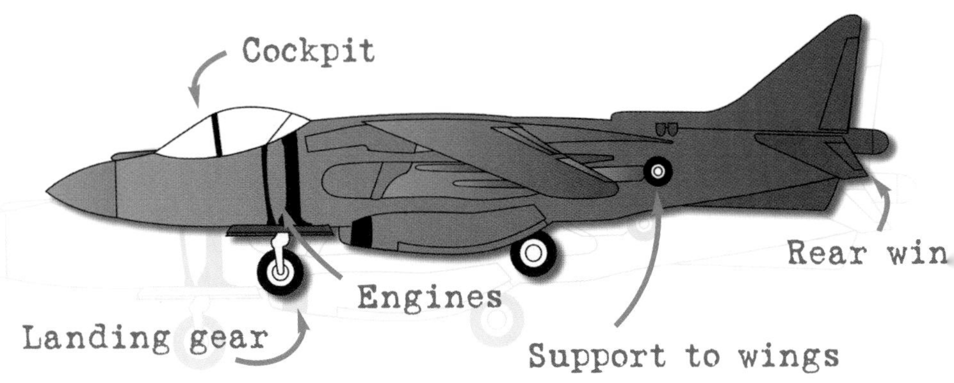

Front view

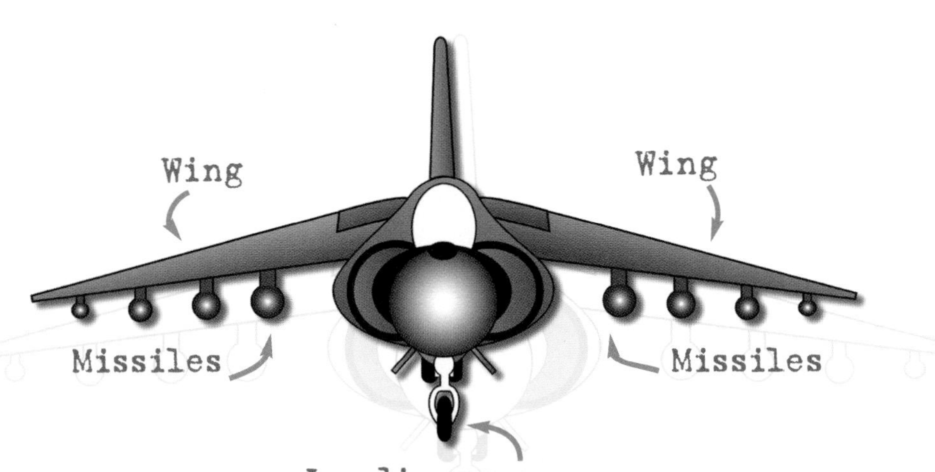

AV-8B Specifications	
Operating Weight Empty:	14,867 lb
Maximum Useful Load:	16,133 lb
Maximum TOGW:	32,000 lb
Maximum External Load Capability: (includes gun and ammo)	13,234 lb
Maximum Speed: (1.0 Mach)	585 kts
Range:	1600 Miles

NEW WORDS

aircraft carrier a large navy ship used as an airport at sea
fuselage the main body of an airplane
hover fly in place
HUD head up display
laser a very bright beam of light
radar (RAdio Detecting And Ranging) an electronic device that sends out signals which bounce off planes, buildings, or ships and return as images on a video screen
rotors spinning blades on top of a helicopter
terrain ground, or the shape of the ground
vertical straight up
viffing vectoring in forward flight
V/STOL vertical, short take-off and landing
WAC weapon aiming computer
wingspan the distance from the tip of one wing to the tip of the other wing of an aircraft

For Further Reading

Badrocke, Mike, and Bill Gunston. *The Illustrated History of McDonnell Douglas Aircraft: From Cloudster to Boeing.* Osceola, WI: Osprey Publications, 1999.

Fraes, Bill Gunston. *Fighter Planes, History Series.* Hauppauge, NY: Barron's Educational Series, Incorporated, 1999.

Schleifer, Jay. *Fighter Planes.* Danbury, CT: Children's Press, 1998.

Sullivan, George. *Modern Fighter Planes.* New York: Facts on File, 1991.

AV-8B Harrier II Plus Joint Program Office
www.av8B.org
This site provides information about the qualities of the AV-8B II. It includes the Harrier's history, pictures, and a video of the aircraft.

Fighter Planes
www.iaehv.nl/users/wbergmns/jets.htm
This site contains a detailed history of fighter planes. It also includes pictures and technical information about more than eighty different fighter planes.

The Navy Fact File
www.chinfo.navy.mil/navpalib/factfile/aircraft/air-av8.html
This is an official site of the U.S. Navy. It has information about different types of military equipment. It also has background facts and a description of the AV-8B Harrier II.

INDEX

INDEX

About the Author

Julie Beyer is a freelance children's book author. She lives in Peachtree City, Georgia, with her husband and three children.